Blue Skies.

John E. Franklin Jr.

Presentation by *BookLeaf Publishing*

Web: www.bookleafpub.com

E-mail: info@bookleafpub.com

ISBN: 9789363310452

First edition 2024

I give thanks and praises to God, who's the head of my life.

To my mom, Lynn Frost, and my late father, John E. Franklin Sr., who loved, raised, and cared for me throughout my life, even during my broken moments.

To my late grandmothers, Vairy Frost and Alice Franklin, who supported me and taught me life lessons about relationships, education, and Christian life.

To my late college professor, Rebecca Belcher-Rankin, and all my writing teachers, who helped me throughout my writing journey and made me a better writer.

To my best friends, Jamarius, Jonavan, and Justin, my inspiration for the poem, "My Best Friend."

To my family, friends, other school teachers, church members, and acquaintances at large who fashion the man I am today, including those who passed away.

And a special thanks to BookLeaf Publishing for publishing my first-ever written work and supporting numerous writers and poets around the world.

ACKNOWLEDGEMENTS

Let me first say thank you to BookLeaf Publishing for helping me complete this poetry book.

Shoutout to Mujtaba Feroz Shah for designing the front and back covers.

Thank you, Roosha Debnath, for editing the manuscript.

A special thank you to my publishing consultant, Priya Reddy, for guiding me and helping me through the publishing process.

And a thank you to you, the reader, for either purchasing this book or investing your time to read this book.

I hope this book will give you encouragement, inspiration, and healing lifelong.

God bless you.

PREFACE

Throughout my life, I've written many poems and works, depicting my own mental struggles and journey towards acceptance and self-transformation. Sharing my personal experiences from childhood to adulthood is one reason I write.

But writing about mental health and self-love wasn't easy. Sometimes, I was afraid to share my dark, pessimistic thoughts because dark themes, like depression or self-destruction, leave a morbid, unpleasant feeling for sensitive readers. It also brought some painful memories of isolation and loneliness I experienced during my school career and personal life. And this is coming from an optimistic kid and a man of faith.

Starting as a teenager, I went through an identity crisis. Dealt with manipulative people and bullies. Took accountability for my toxic, dismissive reactions toward others. Even shared my experiences of depression and grief with close friends and family members who face similar experiences.

After weeks of self-reflection and prayer, I started with twenty-one poems for the #TheWriteAngle challenge, which turned into a fifty-poem poetry book called *Blue Skies*.

From watching Chicago meteorologists like Tom Skilling, Tracy Butler, and the late Jerry Taft, I was in awe of learning about the weather. Fascinated with the stars at night, the power of thunderstorms, and the calmness of a rainy day, I used my imagination to describe my human experiences, my spiritual faith, and my mental struggles in the context of nature, weather, and the universe. I chose the title, *Blue Skies*, because (1) blue is my favorite color and (2) I've always been a kid who enjoys learning about the weather.

The first five poems explore creation, birth, and purpose, using the birth of a star as a metaphor.

The middle forty poems explore the themes of nature, identity, relationships, and depression, revealing personal reflections from my life.

The last five poems explore the themes of death, renewal, and resurrection, mirroring the first five poems based on format, unique style, and juxtaposed ideas.

My self-titled poem summarizes the entire collection in haikus; it focuses on important lessons from each poem, emphasizing the bittersweet beauty of the human journey.

Most poems in this collection are free verse and rhymed. However, other poem formats—haiku, sonnet, prose, chanso, duplex, villanelle, hay(na)ku, etc.—are included.

I hope *Blue Skies* provides you with a genuine yet positive outlook, discovering goodness and serenity in your own life experiences, even those painful moments. I hope you find inspiration and encouragement from a poem or two in this collection. Enjoy.

DISCLAIMER: A few poems in this collection (like "Arctic Trust," "Dark Miracle," & "Dark Thoughts") have sensitive themes and topics triggering for sensitive readers, including bullying, abuse, trauma, depression, and suicidal ideation. Therefore, reader discretion is advised.

Table of Contents

SET I. CREATION

Divine Introduction

God of Life, water
This soul with divinity,
Your cherished treasure.

Invocation of Immanuel

Immanuel, the God who is with me,
Draw yourself to me in this mental jail.
Break these chains, my strongholds, and set me
free.
Lift this black, broken temple, young but frail.
Sober my mind of Depression's cocktail.
Quiet my thoughts. Let my darkest fears cease.
Give me words to speak in precise detail.
Lead me towards the place of joy and peace.

Immanuel, the God who is with me,
Give me guidance, hiking on Cristo's trail.
Give me strength as I pray on bended knee.
Let Your voice sing over me in the gale.
Lead me along the raging seas to sail
Through the storms where Your words command
and seize
The tempest and enemies that assail.
Lead me towards the place of joy and peace.

Immanuel, the God who is with me,
Grant me wisdom to share my broken tale.
Unlock Pandora's box with your faith key
To reveal what's hidden under the veil!
Spill my suffering from Your Holy Grail,
So others can admire Your masterpiece,
I'm a transformed person born from the dale.
Lead me towards the place of joy and peace.

Let the blues skies come, so my lungs inhale
The meadows' breeze for my mental release.
My Immanuel, please help me prevail.
Lead me towards the place of joy and peace.

Bleu Star

Born from dust,
A soul so captivating.
Young, humble model one can trust.
You're an evolving, shining star, so motivating.

Blue star, let your light shine
In this glorious galaxy far away!
You dwell in the starry space where infinite stars
align and intertwine.
Your splendor of constellations shines in the
night sky like the sun during the day.

You radiate your burning power
Beyond a vast galaxy.
Your bright indigo color shines on this dark
hour,
The sweet fragrance and taste of God's glory
and majesty.

Beautiful light of blue,
Be your creative self as you travel through this starry floor.
Folks will try to dim your light or outshine you.
They will exert their energy to destroy you as you walk through God's door.

When you hear folks talk about you in hostile fashion,
Will you exhaust your energy to anger and frustration,
Or be the gentleman who converts your emotions towards heated passion:
A pure pursuit for joy and purpose laid on a firm foundation?

You're the wish a child could ask for.
The story of your journey is their hope.
Impact them with a dream to find their peace and soar
Over this dark void when they reached the string of their rope.

Leave a legacy lasting a million years from now,
For life comes fast for you. Be grateful anyhow.
Be free and merry!
Wear the glory of your supernova you carry.

Blueprints

Blue
Wallpaper painted
In the sky.

It starts with an idea in your imagination,
An outline of plans written in a journal,
A deep passion turned to active manifestation.
A dreamer's delight reveals his adventure, her journey.

How the blueprints reflect the skies' plans for our lives!
We draw blueprints to lay the foundation for sketches to become skyscrapers.
But how divine is the Holy Painter to craft us like pottery, using kintsugi to preserve our glory?

Parchment-made paper keeps dreams alive in
our days of intense fire.
Burnout, rejection, and setbacks keep us from
succeeding or thriving,
But let's return to our first love that made our
lives enjoyable and memorable.

Loosened threads from worn-out blankets and
rugs
Make their debut, fasten in the tapestry of
Heaven's beautiful masterpiece in the sky.
They tell stories of dreamers discovering their
worth and persevering for their eternal treasure.

Rock piles or cairns mark the places we journey
through.
We reach the destination of peace and
tranquility.
Search for a home of comfort, acceptance, and
complete contentment.

Dream big, for your small goals reveal a
God-given, lifelong purpose.
Let your dream be free, for your faith outweighs
the impossibilities.
Know your worth, for fading treasures on Earth
cannot buy your worth or your soul.
Remember who you are, so you find your peace
and healing.

Keep your mind pristine and bright as the star
you wish upon.
Write your affirmations and imprint scriptures
on your hearts, hands, and feet.
Be still in the quietness; let Peace share her
plans to unfold your new life.
Be humble and strengthened in the foundation of
perseverance.

Draw
The blueprints
And dream again.

Joslyn's Lullaby

Would've been our mother and father's love,
A promised daughter from Heaven above,
Child ascended towards them like a dove,
Answered prayer born in our mother's womb.

Yet a chromosome changed from X to Y.
Did God have plans for a star in the sky?
Blue star incarnated into a guy.
It was an unexpected miracle.

Would you forgive me for taking your place?
A child conceived by God's mercy and grace.
Comfort me, my friend, with your warm
embrace,
From our mother's arms to the reaper's tomb.

Don't know why God chose this indigo star.
But I will love my mother, my all-star,
Honor my father's name, my tattooed scar.
We are Joslyn, handsome and beautiful.

Answered prayer born in our mother's womb.
It was an unexpected miracle.
From our mother's arms to the reaper's tomb,
We are Joslyn, handsome and beautiful

SET II. NATURE

Morning Blues

I woke up on this rough morning, staring at the ceiling, feeling blue.
The sun rises, but a million thoughts keep me in bed, just going through.

Past mistakes and traumas cause my headaches, feeling vertigo.
Future predictions tell an unfortunate fate: watching my life hit a new low.

Why should I rise for another day, feeling frustrated?
Or I'm unable to cope with my emotions, making things complicated?

How long should I live feeling unwanted?
The warm comforters on my bed hug me when my surroundings are cold and haunted?

I can’t stand the light in my window, feeling judged or criticized,
Questioning whether I’m a kid despised or prized?

I wish my reality was fun as the dreams I discovered, feeling cheerful,
I wished I embraced my creativity and identity without my inner child being fearful.

I want to become my true self, forever feeling appreciated.
I pray my soul can find peace as I wake from my bed refreshed and motivated.

Maybe it’s the butterflies flying inside my stomach, feeling queasy.
Morning sickness, emotional breakdowns, anxiety, or are these annoying allergies making me sneezy?

Am I accepting these morning blues, feeling depressed?
Here comes the thought dump to empty, vomiting thoughts to wake up refreshed and decompressed?

I'll take a few minutes to breathe before I rise, feeling scared
Of the morning blues where my irrational fears kept my body and mind impaired.

I'll relive the moments I could experience, escape, and enjoy again, feeling content.
I'll concentrate on my power to control what's deep within: the dark emotions I'm ready to relent.

Liberate yourself, my soul, from the morning blues, feeling adequate or ashamed.
You have purpose within you, this affirmation I have proclaimed.

Peaceful Lake

Here I am,
Gazing at the sunrise.
The morning light has come.

Here lie the beautiful meadows I rest on,
Stargazing as it changes from black to blue.
It's a glorious display to behold.

Here lies the glistering lake nearby,
Kissing the sky as the sun rises from the
horizon.
A love story retold during the creation of Earth.

Here lie the birds, resting near a tree,
Singing a tune for the animals to sing along.
Harmony and peace married near the shore.

Here lies a couple,
Resting in a hammock watching the sunrise,
Eating beauty and gratitude, a tasty breakfast for
God's creation.

Here's where salmon swim,
Jumping in the air with joy.
A journey finished after a lifelong challenge of
perseverance.

Here lie the mountains,
Remembering how they became hills.
A testimony of consistent climbing to reach
Heaven with their persistent peaks.

Here I am,
Enjoying my rest before my day begins.
What a peaceful start, resting on this peaceful
lake!

Coral Salmon

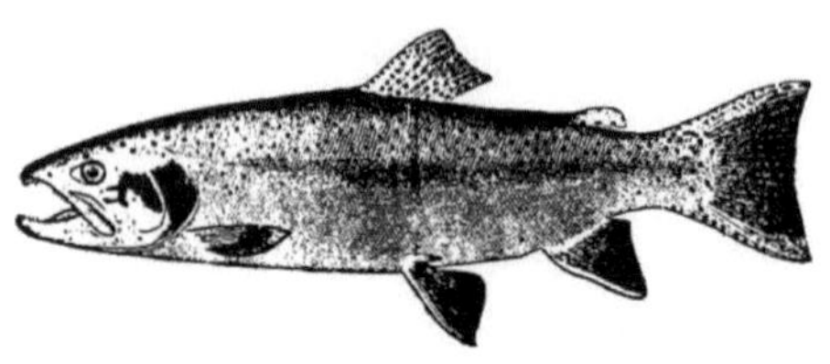

Here's a tale that's real, not fake,
Nature's story to keep your mind awake.
A fish who persevered,
A hero we revered
From the shores of this peaceful lake.

A coral salmon, born near the mountains, swims from her freshwater habitat.
Her peach color, crafted in flesh, fades to gray scars.
A home feast, her parents' blessings, give her strength for the journey.
Now, she's ready to travel to the oceans.

This coral salmon, here in the Pacific, swims until I reach her saltwater world.
Her silver color, designed from glory, appears on her skin.
This tough trip, her migration, becomes her challenge for life.
Now, she's maturing to swim up the mountain.

The coral salmon, resting below the sea, swims
up the Alaskan river.
Her opaque color, transparent and special,
reveals her determination.
The obstacles, waterfalls, and predators form to
stop her.
Now, she's persevering to face the river current.

The coral salmon, jumping up the waterfall,
swims through the obstacles.
Her red color, vibrant in hue, tells of her
struggles.
The testimony, exhaustion, and motivation are
stories she tells.
Now, she's closer to making the river her resting
place.

Our salmon, reaching towards freshwater, swims
to the river.
Her coral color, beautiful and rare, disappears
under the gravel.
Our baby, admired and altruistic, sacrificed her
life for everyone.
Now, she's giving her all for her descendants and
the ecosystem.

A coral salmon, resting beyond the shores,
swims towards the sun.
Her white color, dripped in purity, shines above
the waters.
A unique fish, our champion, persevered to find
her home.
Now, she's the lesson for us to persevere through
our own obstacles.

Life is not a piece of cake,
It’s filled with challenges that’ll make you
quake.
But stay strong against what you feared,
Let your mind, freed and cleared,
Choose the destined path–a choice you must
make.

Innovative Flight

I imagined clouds walking through the sky.
They move to our quiet neighborhood
To show kindness and cheer us up.
How they greet us like children,
Encouraging us to
Think big in our minds,
A truth we learn
From a clear,
Big, blue
Sky.

Innovative imagination, a
Child's gift from God to believe in a
True dream no one can take away.
Ground to the ceiling, we dream
To reach above the stars,
The ambitions to
Rise t'wards the sky
and, like a
cloud, touch
It.

Clouds move to greet us in a clear, blue sky.
A child's dream: to reach the sky and touch it.

Sunday's Delight

What a time to enjoy Sunday's delight:
A sundae mixed with God's love, peace, and
grace
Best served under Nature's cozy daylight.

Come to church, needing hope for this week's
plight.
Enter God's presence, seeking His embrace.
What a time to enjoy Sunday's delight.

Family and friends visit by noonlight,
Fellowship and music, all commonplace,
Best served under Nature's cozy daylight.

I take a sabbatical rest to write
My thoughts on a notebook, my safe space.
What a time to enjoy Sunday's delight!

Resting on Sunday, my peaceful highlight,
Is a homemade meal with a smiley face,
Best served under Nature's cozy daylight.

Sunday's a good day! It's a peaceful sight
To rest with God and empty my headspace.
What a time to enjoy Sunday's delight,
Best served under Nature's cozy daylight.

Rainy Moments

The clouds cover the sky to create the mood.
Rainy moments I remember locked in solitude.

When the rain pours, and the sky turns gray,
I shelter in and reflect on my darkest day.

Tears drop like hail, grieving for the people I
lost.
Love is a beautiful action, but sacrifice is its
hefty cost.

The defiant downpours knock on my
windowpane.
But I refuse to answer it; I've had enough rain.

I’m tired of seeking people to hear my voice,
As if the storm within me was a choice.

I rather let this storm rage before the break of
dawn,
That a stronger man will emerge with his dark
emotions gone.

The storm turns a blue, clear sky dark like
midnight
With its lightning as the sole source of light.

Smell the cool, fresh air, pushing through the
humid and heated ground,
As the violent storm makes its presence with an
eerie yet horrid sound.

Here comes its thunderous voice, echoing
through the sky.
The winds scream like a powerful tantrum,
explosive as an emotional breakdown, and loud
as a war cry.

Let the tornado destroy this broken home.
I’ll start over in the wreckage to find my solace
and shalom.

What you do when you're isolated in your own storm,
Watching its destructive power destroy your soul like locusts in a swarm?

Thunderstorms scared me as a kid until I respected its power.
As I matured, I disciplined my emotions, a storm tamed into a drizzling shower.

Soothed my anger with the cool rain before it became a wildfire
Relieved my anxieties with tabletop games and journaling before I popped like a flat tire.

When the storm subsides into a calm overcast,
I'll submerge my body in the rain for Heaven to heal an outcast.
The tears from my eyes will merge with the rain showers,
Unsaid burdens relieved as Heaven's cleansing rain drenched the flowers.

Let the smoothing, calm drizzle melt away my sorrow,
So, I can hope for a brighter day tomorrow.

Thunderstorm

Born as a fluffy cumulus cloud,
Full of joy and happiness.
But I can form into a cumulonimbus cloud,
Full of rage and power.

I'm as calm as a peaceful lake,
Resting near the grass in silence.
But I'm chaotic as a tsunami wave,
Frustrated with folks, ill-tempered.

I can choose positivity
To think of better days ahead.
I can choose negativity
To speak of pessimistic thoughts unsaid.

I can choose to become your ally,
A die-hard friend till the end.
I can choose to become your enemy,
A persevering rival till friendships end.

I can forgive when you make a mistake,
I find hope in your repentance.
But I'll never forget what you've done,
I build boundaries for my deliverance.

I can love you with unconditional love,
Be everything you want me to be.
But dare cross the line,
And I'll be what you don't want to see.

I can cover you on a rainy day,
Showering you with love for your tears.
But I can damage you during severe weather,
Destroying everything because of my irrational fears.

I can speak kind words
To encourage you one day.
I can speak dark thoughts
That concern you another day.

I can't control the thunderstorm inside of me,
Allowing life circumstances to depress me.
But I can control the thunderstorm inside of me,
Letting my suppressed emotions go to free me.

I'm a cumulonimbus on a hard day,
But I will always be a fluffy cloud, just not today.
A range of powerful emotions can form a storm,
But Peace whispers to me, even during a thunderstorm.

Evening Dew

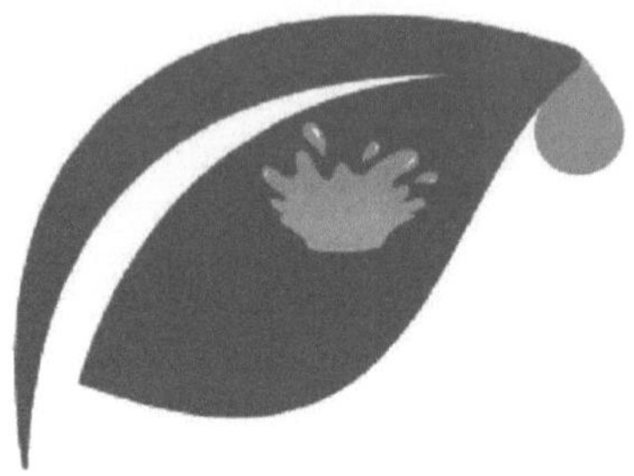

Look at this blade of grass with evening dew.
It keeps water. Condenses the excess.
Like dew, knowledge and faith rest upon you.
Don’t drink too much or too fast to impress
Folks still toiling and learning to progress.
Be humbled with what you have now to thrive
In a drought, your mind will help you survive.

The Eclipse of Favor

The mystery of blessings buried,
Eclipsed in favor, an undeserved gift.

Favor is an eclipsed gift we don't deserve.
It's a feared spiritual phenomenon.

But don't fear this special, spiritual gift.
Focus your glasses to see the glory of this
phenomenon.

Raise your drinking glasses to celebrate the
glory of the eclipse.
Stars and men, behold the total solar eclipse!

Stars and women, I give you the lunar eclipse!
They're sacred twins God favored for
excellence.

They're divine twins God predestined for greatness.
Day and night, we're blessed with nature's gifts.

Night and day, we receive God's loving grace,
The secret blessings uncovered.

Every Blue Moon

Through a telescope,
Hailey's comet and her starry friends soar
through the endless universe.
The moon changes her mood as she goes
through her phases.
Rainbows teach us of a promise of peace in a
thunderstorm.
The northern lights dance in a clear night sky.
Every blue moon, nature's phenomena happen,
Never experienced through a digital format.

In our eyes,
We watched our children grow towards adults as
we age.
Handed our mentors and teachers their flowers
to smell.
Seen generational curses broken from the cradle
to the grave.

Hosted parties to reminisce about the days of childhood fun, tasteful delights, and nostalgic treasures.
Special moments with our family and friends became our favorite movies.
Every blue moon, human experiences are beautiful when we cherish the people we love while we have a chance.

In our minds,
Déjà vu helps us relive memories to overcome our present circumstances.
Dreams open the doors of our passions, bigger than our fantasies.
The presence of deceased friends and family comforts us through our grievances.
Creativity and spiritual inspiration collide to form a "Heaven on Earth" experience.
Thoughts hang out on a train, traveling through a limited space where unlimited possibilities thrive.
Every blue moon, our minds take us on adventures where reality searches for hope in a dark world.

In our hearts,
We sacrifice to protect the people we care about.
Make room for what's fresh and precious instead of what's trending and popular.

Look for love that's genuine and prevailing.
Paint and picture the inner beauty of our souls.
Search for the right path using God's light.
Every blue moon, our hearts discover home
when we're lost and stuck in our broken vessels.

From my point of view,
Black coal transforms into diamonds.
Poor rags fashioned into new clothes.
Seeds grow into gardens of radiant,
sweet-smelling wildflowers.
A new, positive outlook on life and oneself
becomes truth.
I hope it doesn't take every blue moon to
appreciate these precious moments.

Though we're changing like moon phases,
Let not the beautiful, precious moments become
relevant only on every blue moon,
For they are rare, lifetime stories,
Blessings never forgotten.
Never forget about what you have,
Every blue moon, they will disappear, unless we
acknowledge their value now.

SET III. IDENTITY

Royal Crown

Mobility of freedom and love,
Accountability, perfection,
Totality of pure holiness,
Utility of expense and trust,
Responsibility of masses,
Eligibility beyond race.

A royal golden crown designed and crafted,
Originated from the Heavens.
You chose a lost, low lad from trenches,
A broken man coming from nothing,
Left rejected from society.

Lord, come to my aid and hear my prayer:
Receive as your child who pleads mercy.
Open my eyes to accept this honor.
Will I mess up my chance,
or will my nobility shines brighter than this
Shiny, golden crown I wear on my head?

Reflections

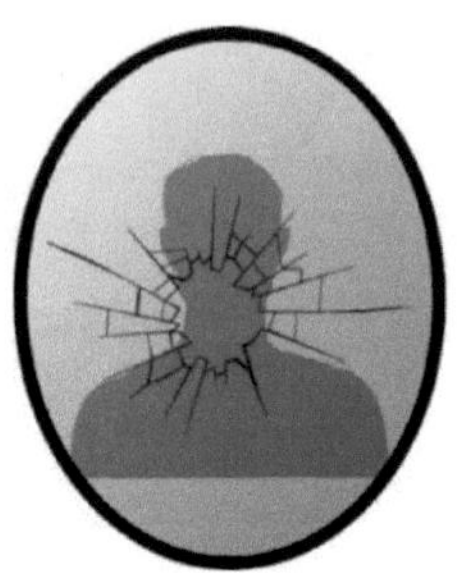

Look in the mirror.
Tell me what you see.

I see myself in a bathroom mirror.
He's looking straight at me.
My identical twin mimics me,
Boosts my self-esteem,
Increases my charisma,
And reinvigorates this broken vessel.

He stares, but what he doesn't see is a broken soul.
The blinds cover up the windows of my eyes.
The condensing tears fog up my eyes on a dreary, drizzling day.
How can he find value through the clouded thoughts of false expectations and prideful assertions?

I'm like a Disney Princess,
Staring at the water to search for the handsome soul inside.
But I'm not like Narcissus,
For my reflection is what I despise most.

How can he see me as a professional, tough man when I'm crying like a child?
Why is it hard to hold emotions and tears with a heart broken?
I bear the scars and scrapes on my skin,
But the disease of insecurity and anxiety lives daily, lifelong.

Yet, I look in the mirror,
Admire this heavenly masterpiece.
No one can become like me,
Nor do I envy what I can't be.

Time to reflect on my life,
But I can't reminisce about my past for too long.
Today, I remind myself to take my time.
Step by step, I will run this race.
Day by day, making it through.
Breathe in the beauty within.
Breathe out the brokenness you speak.

Look in the mirror.
Tell me what you see.

I see myself walking through life under my shadow.
He's there, heading in my direction.
It's my inner child following his future.
Encourages himself to fight on,
Affirms what he believes as truth about himself,
And discovers his reflection is him.
Yes, my reflection is him, the one I learned to love and appreciate.

Comfortable Blue

Pair of jeans and shoes, covered in blue.
A white T-shirt and black socks to add to this clothing affair.
Scared to walk through the hallways of school to make my social debut.
Butterflies fluttered inside me. Will they accept me?
Wish me luck or pray for my breakthrough.
I'm seeking a comrade who calls me his or her friend,
Makes me comfortable to become myself, not like a celebrity or a fashion guru,
But an everyday friend who's there.
Even through rainy days and tough times, I can be a brother, genuine and true.

Cool Kid

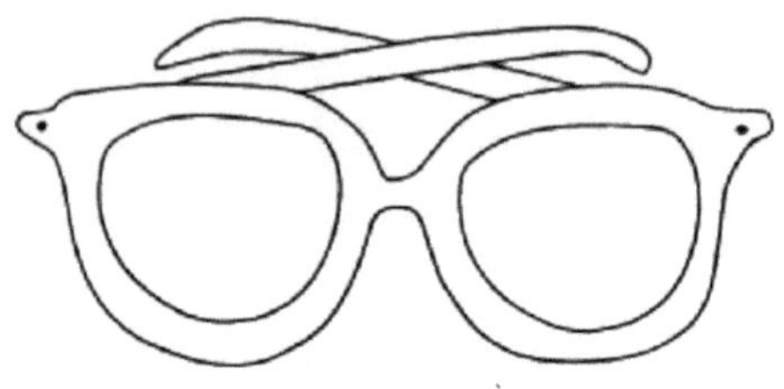

Who's the cool kid on the block,
With the black shades, the stylish jacket, and fresh kicks posing like a stern rock?
He's the fly cat with his signature written in chalk near the dock.
The sly fox with the drip who impresses the flock.

I wasn't always the cool kid
In a society of nerds, popular teens, and jocks.
Their cliché status quo and groupthink are mid.
That's why teenagers hide themselves in places with combination locks.

Yet, I buried my identity to hide my existence.
Clothe my skin with a costume.
I gain likes, compliments, and friends for being fake to feed my subsistence.

It's a risk of showing my true self in a crowded room.

Recognition became my desperation.
To feel wanted became my desire.
But the rejection and pressure became my condemnation.
To lose myself became my prison, surrounded by barbed wire.

I became the kid who sat by himself for lunch,
The quiet teen who stuttered words, afraid to stand up for himself.
Losing every mental battle is a gut punch,
Falling from this societal shelf.

Was it true of their opinions, gossip, and side commentaries,
Or the stern glares and sharp lips that pierced my soul?
Connect me to an encouraging choir of canaries
To silence those who continue to troll.

I'm not as athletic as a jock with muscular arms
Or chiseled abs on the bench press.
I'm not a prom king with charms,
Nor the nerd who takes pride in a game of chess.

But can't I be the boring, multilayered human being,
Living for a cause to seek my heavenly goal above?
Or are you the audience sightseeing
And booing me when I speak of love.

Should I care about being canceled for not sticking to your status quo,
Or too woke to love than deal with your exhausting hate?
Do you judge me for being a vigorous man who learns to grow,
Or criticize me for being a man who cares about lightening this emotional weight?

I have nothing to lose in this social media fight,
Proving to trolls who cannot love themselves, a truth they tried to bury?
Never needed popularity, followers, or trends to fight for what's right.
I gained friends, names written in my heart's archives in my private library.

I'm not a cool kid because I chose this fate,
But I've become comfortable in my turquoise estate.
Should I live a lie, so folks can hold my wings to amputate,

Or risk dying to discover a new identity that will never deteriorate?

Ran Myself Away

I ran myself away to the frontier,
Letting the inner kid go in my life.
Losing my love pierced my heart like a knife.
Lost my innocent heart each passing year.
I bled tears because my pain turned severe,
Cause of betrayal like a scorned wife
Or a husband bearing domestic strife.
God, I wish I could fly and disappear.

Inner man, let not your emotions rage.
You can't return to your past self again.
Free yourself from this emotional cage.
You must fight for yourself. Work through the pain.
Return to the home to write your next page,
Your future's now handwritten in each vein.

Hoodies & Masks

I hid my identity,
Covering my bruises and scars in a navy sweater.
Masked my face of scrapes and burns to the third degree.
How I kept my heart in a treasure box,
Hidden with a lock but threw away the key.

Will I discover who I am, my genuine self,
When others make me feel like an outsider on Zacchaeus' tree?
Or is the perfect weather
To undress the layers in this masque to reveal the true me?

Jeans of Faith

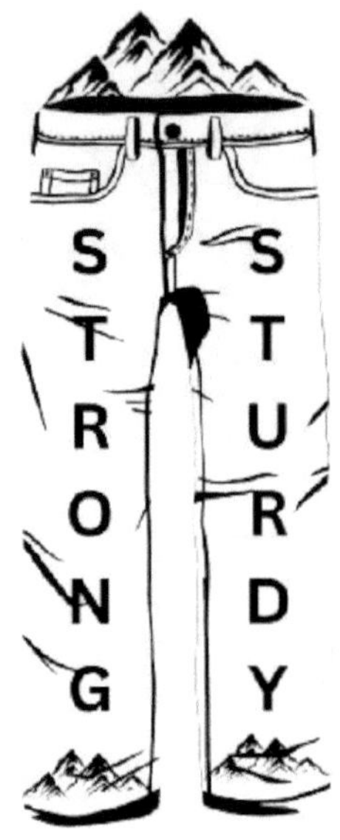

Denim fit,
Sturdy foundation,
Blue clothing that moves mountains.
Everyday wear, well-stitched for hard days.
Whether cut, dirty, or faded, they're like hope.
Persistent, even when they tear. Their
Durable material
Made sturdy and strong
In tough times.

ICON

I'm iconic, man, the grand trendsetter,
The handsome lad, dressed in a black sweater.
New attraction of an amusement park,
I'm a historic national landmark,
Repping the Windy City, born and raised.
Your slander of my name keeps me unfazed.
Practiced my grand entrance to reach my goal:
Escaped from the pit you called a hellhole.
I'm the brand, homemade and original,
A prophet whose words are sharp, never dull,
Authentic, genuine, the real deal.
See my true self through the layers I peel:
Discernment and intuition, my smarts.
I protect fragile, vulnerable hearts,
Before evil, vile people get head starts,

Using harsh, piercing words, sharper than darts.
These haters and critics stroke my ego.
Their hate spreads, latches like a serpigo.
I'm a chill dude, unproblematic wine,
Until they're one problem plus ninety-nine.
Honored with a dope platform and spotlight.
Faced my emotional storm at midnight.
Opened eyes for a future groundbreaking,
Discovered faith and hope so earthshaking.
Overcame barriers on the ceiling.
Freed myself of my chains to find healing.
Critics censored and canceled my vision,
Their erasure newspaper, revision
It's just drama and gossip, all the same,
It's the price for recognition and fame.
Worked and earned my twenty-four hours of fame,
Living the spotlight under a new name.
Didn't care to join their own treehouse club
'Til rejection came; I became a snub.
They disrespected them 'til I shut up.
I flex in silence to dodge their setup.
They pierce my blue heart with their 6-inch heels.
Stomp with their black Timbs made of rubber wheels.
I'm trashed like a hand-me-down on the street,
But like a phoenix, I'll rise, my top feat,
Out the pit like Dave, the grave like Jesus

They'll never be me; they're never like us.
The CEO of I, myself, and me
Advanced to a new height, level, degree
I ain't your average celebrity,
This indigo star formed from space debris.
Jaws dropped in awe at the paparazzi.
Dropped the mic like the GOAT living carefree.
Keep your standing ovation or applause.
God has the last word, the completed clause.
Don't give encores to those who ain't believed.
Nothing to prove of the goals I achieved.
I followed my God, who's holy and pure,
When my frail heart needed strength to endure.
But I'm here today, grown, wise, and mature.
What a thrilling, unprecedented tour!
Let's create another path to success,
A long-enduring journey to progress,
For what money can't buy, what work can't
earn:
My life-changing purpose I will soon learn.

VIP

You are what I call valuable. That's why I
invited you all to this party.

You all stayed in the valleys, the icebergs, or the
pits,
Because they called you hopeless victims,
isolated foreigners, and poor folks.
No one cared to value your insight to create a
better world.
How their vanity took away your innocence,
even when you showed them love.
How they used you, ignored you, and left you
with baggage of pain.
They saw you as a number, a volatile individual
with no potential.
Woe to the folks we respected and loved, but
turned out arrogant, ignorant, and pompous.

Have we lost our vigor to reach those isolated?
Have we not opened our doors for our neighbors
to feel welcomed?

Our vengeful vendettas or social ignorance stop
us from loving each other.
Never let our victimizers influence us to become
like them!

My brothers and sisters, we built a community
from voices who needed inspiration and passion.
Volunteers ventured out to show integrity and
pure love to the left out.
Families verbalized their support and insight
without pushing others away.
Global networks vocalized a positive message of
imitating a vision of a peaceful world.
Churches invested in veracity, holy intuition,
and a safe presence for God and His people.

How our vigorous intelligence perfected our
path
Towards a beautiful vision where we feel
included and peaceful
In a world where the VIPs include the
insignificant and the poor.

You are our VIPs, valuable, intelligent people.
Use your voice of intellect and passion to invite
the isolated to the family.
Let's make it a vacation near the islands or along
the plateaus.

Search through the valleys, icebergs, and the deep pits.
Share the hope of victory you found to inspire others.
Tell them how much they are valued, included, and prized as an integral part of our family.

My friends, know your value and worth when others call you insignificant or pathetic.
You are valuable, and you're always welcomed to our party.
You're our valent special guests, our innovative co-workers, and our genuine pals,
Who experienced a void of isolation and persecution from society's ladder and hierarchy.
Now let's voice our response, illuminating our light around the world for the people to find hope.

Living Water

You are living water,
A pristine river
On the mountain top.
Revival is what you deliver.

You are a role model,
An influence on generations.
Be an example for your children,
A leader for the nations.

You are a dreamer.
Imagine what you want to be.
Whatever path you choose,
I hope it becomes reality; I decree.

You are a hero,
Saving yourself from the muck.
It's okay not to be strong every time.
Everyone needs a hero when they are stuck.

You are enough,
A saying repeated but underappreciated.
Connect your soul to the river
To receive the blessings donated.

Don't be ashamed of your anointing,
Your God-given abilities and favor.
God qualifies the unqualified,
Giving hope for when faith and expectations waver.

Let your emotions not dictate your decisions,
Though folks persecute you by tongue.
Let no one discourage you, friend,
Because you're young.

Keep believing in make-believe.
Cater to your imagination.
Give your inner child a chance
To build your life on a firm foundation.

No one will save you from the storm,
But you can be your own saving miracle.
What people spoke evil and caused you an impossibility,
You overcame and solidified your victory with a testimony, hysterical and satirical.

You are a living gospel for Heaven's greatest story,
A message of hope for God's glory.
Let your life be like living water in every frontier
To water the seeds of wisdom, far and near.

SET IV. RELATIONSHIPS

PSALM 2025

To the chief Musician. A Psalm of John.

Praise the LORD of the skies, the creatures of
air, land, and sea!
Let every breath within speak of His goodness,
A life full of blessing and favor, raining from
Heaven above.

See how His mighty hand formed the planets
and stars,
How He paints the for Nature to awe at t
Such a sight over the horizon!
The plants and trees give their first fruits to Him.
The robins join the heavenly chorus with the
morning sound of nature,
And the owls hoot along with the evening
sounds.

How He cares for His creation with
unconditional love and provision,
And how He gives hope for us through His word
and vision.

What has not the Lord done for us
To show His faithful love and compassion
towards us?
Look how He used the mundane things we take
for granted
To remind us to be grateful for what we have
and what He gives us.

Do not fear or be dismayed.
Does not the Father know what we need before
we ask,
See our future before it arrives today,
Plan before we see it unfold,
Or test our faith before we understand the
lesson?

How the LORD brought us through our storms.
Oh, how they rage, yet He gave us hope to
persevere.
Oh, how He rescued us from a swarm of
enemies,
And blow them away in the wind, His mighty
breath.
How he came to our aid in our dark times,

Even when we contemplated surrendering or giving up.
He built us for the tough times
To thrive through our desert experiences,
Transitioning us from the wilderness
To the restful place near the meadows,
Forever resting near living water,
Forever feeding on pure fruit in His gardens.

Praise the LORD of the skies, the creatures of air, land, and sea!
Let our praise speak of His wonderful acts of kindness,
And His faithful love, blooming and growing from the Earth below.

Lead us through whatever comes towards us
And guide us through until we reach Paradise.

Let Heaven and Earth praise Your excellent name,
Our Immanuel and Yeshua.

My Best Friend

I called you my best friend,
Cause you became my first friend I met.
In a strange place where anxieties flourish or end,
You became a risk, a choice I'll never regret.

But I wasn't your best friend,
Because I couldn't trust anyone to care for me.
Bullied, traumatized, and singled out, lying in my isolated den,
Waiting for the perfect person to teach me about love like I was a newbie.

Yet, I was the naïve friend,
Arguing over foolish, mundane mistakes.
Held my emotions until the dam burst in the deep end,
And resisted opening my mouth, unable to heal from these consistent aches.

I became your silent friend.
Silent treatments and miscommunication build the walls between us.
I blamed you for what you could not defend,
Yet, I blame myself for not giving you a chance to discuss.

I hate becoming your friend.
Embarrassed you with random outbursts I needed to outgrow.
Left you hurt and broken as our friendship reached a dead end.
You became the best thing I prayed for, but I don't deserve you, mi amigo.

Maybe it's me not being your best friend.
How wrong of me, inconsiderate of your feelings. when my anger and depression arose..
Now hearing your story, I send
A letter of remorse and sympathy translated from my tears, written in prose.

Yet, I hope I can become a better friend,
Trusting you again when it's hard to trust others,
Accepting criticism, even when it's me you
could offend,
And redeeming a broken relationship between
spiritual brothers.

Will you let me be your friend?
Let me be a lighthouse whose light will never
dim,
The brother you can depend on till the very end,
A mature gentleman who honors and treasures
you as a dear friend to him?

You were my best friend.
You cared for me when I was depressed.
I hope one day you'll see this friendship I will
contend,
Fighting for you and a brotherly bond that's
coalesced.

I want to be your best friend,
From kids enjoying each other's company and
presence,
To teens supporting each other's dreams from
beginning to end.
We'll become fine, young men, treasuring our
friendship in God's eternal pleasance.

Blue Light

Under the blue light,
I gazed upon your aura, so inviting and bright.
You're my comforter on a dark night.
Being with you is such a delight.

Your presence keeps me secure.
Your touches, so tender and pure.
Your kisses become the ticket to a grand tour,
Taking me on a trip where love can endure.

I dance with you to slow jams on the dance floor,
The beats and rhythm of the music, counting one, two, three, four.
Dissonance is our harmony when we rage war.
Yet, you're a worthy partner I'll fight and adore.

I don't drink, but I'm drunk on your love.
You give me goosebumps I never get rid of.
You are protective of me like a baseball glove.
You're the angel God sent, descending to me like a dove.

When I'm naked, vulnerable to share my deep secrets and pain,
You comfort and console me to keep me sane.
I'm comfortable with you in bed because you relieve my migraine.
You treat me with patience and care, always humane.

You hold my hand to tell the world I'm yours,
A piece of your heart manifested into a living treasure not sold in stores.
Every day's a trip with you, outdoors.
Yet, I'm excited about our sensual, intimate night adventures indoors.

Our souls become one, concealed and protected in a ring.
We become lifelong friends from summer to spring.
We became full-time lovers, using our love languages to stroke every love string.
Now we've grown older, blessed with the fruits of generational blessings and offspring.

Oh, how I remember the day we met in the dark
blue light.
Love became more than a mere sight.
You became my lover that night,
And now, we'll enjoy this special moment
tonight.

Pink Lemonade

You are a fresh glass of pink lemonade.
Combined enrichment of sweet, sour taste.
The yellow sun shines on your face.
Pink fabrics cover your body, which is Heaven made.

You are like a morning cup of coffee.
Mi armoire, preparato latte macchiato.
Mi amor está en mi mente despertándome como un espresso.
You're my love language of warmth, like a hot cup of tea.

You're my refreshing Italian ice on a summer's day.
How our vision of simplicity and authenticity mix well like a fruit smoothie.
You cool my anxieties like my morning iced green tea.
You're the cool friend I need to talk to at the café.

You dance on my taste buds with seasonings and spices, a meal worth the price.
A spicy yet savory experience of love and passion.
You're my five-course meal, tantalizing my cravings in high fashion,
A satisfying aftertaste blessed me with second helpings and another slice.

You're my pink lemonade, sour and sweet,
An espresso to cheer me up when life looks bleat,
A cold drink to ease my fears, even my temper in high heat,
A five-star restaurant experience full of mystery recipes and tasty treats.

Liability

I trusted you with all my heart and soul.
I consider you a genuine friend.
But I'm a liability, your goal.

You're a reliable source to depend,
But you're a leech, sucking my life and joy.
You drain my soul until my tragic end.

Took advantage of a genuine boy
Who looked out for you when you hit tough times.
How far will you use me as your playtoy?

I'm collateral damage for your crimes.
Your asset when you're in trouble, in need.
Stolen ATM for nickels and dimes.

I showed you love, but you called me a weed,
You took my crops and suffocated me,
Took my private space, so I won't be freed.

Your annoying sting, sharper than a bee,
My reminder of my foolish done deed:
Trusting exploiters to eat off my tree.

I question myself if I should stay kind.
I'm a con man's type–a rare, naïve find.
I trusted you with all my heart and soul
But I'm a liability, your goal.

Arctic Trust

Can't stand this arctic trust of unsure connection.
Gave me an icy stare, a state of dejection.
I questioned my actions and words that left you mad.
Yet you refused to speak to me, leaving me sad.
How could you play with my emotions like a game,
Hoping you win a prize to leave me in my shame?

I tried becoming your friend and helping you out,
But you returned the favor to use me for clout.
I became your next victim, a broken kid trapped.
Innocence and vulnerability kidnapped.
Used God and faith to justify your mean manners.
You're the bully who gaslighted me on banners.

How long will you ruin my life with cold winters?
Forced yourself in and give me frostbite and splinters.
Do you still patronize me for my skin color,
While trying to pollute this heart of a scholar?
Or will you choose to disturb the peace in my mind,
Until I end my life or choose a life unkind?

Fell on the line, thinking I was gentle and weak.
You called me names from the valley and mountain peak.
Is it your choice to make me feel worse than I am?
Mocked me 'til I self-destruct. Never gave a damn!
Don't blame me for sleeping outside in a snowstorm!
Never home, resting with a friend who is lukewarm.

I am done with you and this scammed relationship,
My life's under new management and leadership.
Sorting emotional baggage to lose my grudge,
Relinquishing control to God, our Divine Judge.
I will forgive you if it means healing from you.

But I'll never forget! I'm a man you can't screw.

Let this dark, toxic chapter of my life now end!
I pray I'm healed to become someone else's friend.
Sick of dealing with grown bullies who won't give up
Using others to satisfy their greedy cup.
I became the bullied kid, silent, soft, and scared.
Now, I'm the loud voice with a testimony shared.
Let me feel this hurt alone, so I can unwind,
Hoping to leave those who treat me like crap behind.

Synergy and Serenity

Search for synergy and serenity.
Quiet my soul to find healing again.

Speak out loud, my love, to heal your pain.
Watch your words before you speak to me.

Think before you say a word to me,
Lest you block this river of love from flowing.

Open your lakes of authentic compassion.
Hug me with all your power and your strength.

Cuddle with me, vulnerable and weak.
We celebrate our similarities, yet,

We argue over our differences, but
Let's compromise to build our friendship.

Let us strengthen our relationship
To gain synergy and serenity.

The Quill Pen & The Coaster

Quill pen, write what I imagine and dream,
Let the ideas form in my brainstorm.
Here in this quiet, cozy room, so warm,
Pour your inspiration like a small stream,
Flowing on paper, my rough drafts transform
Into a masterpiece, breaking the norm,
As creativity builds self-esteem.

Coaster, you hold the inner thoughts I write,
Help me discover words I could not say.
Let your blue ink flow possibilities.
Your wisdom will guide me through this long
plight.
Let inspiration come my way each day
'Til I exhausted my abilities.

Roots and Branches

Our trees birth, from the branches and the roots,
Relationships we build along the way.
Our best friends, and our loved ones, bear pure fruits,
Our foundation, upbringing, and pathway.
They stamped their love in our dresses and suits.
Oh, how we miss their presence every day,
Yet their wisdom is firm, like winter boots.
Remember their love on tough days and pray.

We're rooted in the company we keep.
Let go of the dead branches and their weight!
It's the company we keep will dig deep
To steal our resources at a slow rate.
How much longer will your fragile heart weep
To learn they won't change? They just lacerate!
Folks stay in your life, so you cannot sleep.
True friends are the roots that build your estate.

Cut the branches so you can move toward
A journey of inner healing well spent.
Let go of anger and grudges you've stored
Within your soul. Do forgive and repent,
For the tongue is our sharp, double-edged sword.
We're judged for what we said and what we
meant,
Responsible for who enters our horde,
Power to end our bonds with a deep dent.

Inner circle, company, bonds, friendships
Are the deep roots and branches that carry
Heavy baggage from our relationships:
Insecurities that we must bury,
Life is an endless cycle of field trips,
A social rollercoaster that's scary.
Let the dead branches fall, though each one rips.
But your genuine bonds keep you merry.

SELF

How we reach the mountains we climb
Hike through the valleys for meaning.
The truth is we work overtime,
Living a life so demanding.
How people strip one from his heart,
Throw insults at her like a dart.
But the world cannot define U,
Unless you let it define you.
Don't rush life toward the fast lane,
Run your path, a lifelong pursuit,
To redefine yourselves again.

I feel like this truth is a crime.
We're jealous and overweening
To put others down for a dime,
Comparisons intervening
On our growth. We're put on a chart,
Tested, assessed who's rich or smart.
How we struggle with peer review,

Scared of the flaws we can't undo?
Have we lost the growth we obtain?
It's a miraculous breakthrough
To redefine ourselves again.

Why do we cheat ourselves full-time?
Burden ourselves, quarantining
Over flaws and spots we call grime,
Seeking doctors for deep cleaning.
We made bad paths for a restart.
Low self-esteem ruined pureart.
Damage ourselves without a clue
'Til we don't recognize what's true
About ourselves. Do we maintain
The lessons, truths that pulled us through?
Let's redefine ourselves again!

Ignore the social paradigm
And cling to a hope we're leaning,
Finding lovers who sing and rhyme
To songs thought of, not machining.
We search for a true counterpart,
But we must break the bonds apart.
Toxic bonds put true love in queue
'Til we can't see love in full view.
Let our hearts pour down like the rain,
Seeds planted on Love Avenue,
As we define ourselves again.

We must not waste this precious time.
We must begin our spring cleaning.
Don't worry if we passed our prime,
We're designed from God's silk-screening,
Masterpieces, well-crafted art.
His creation's not a spare part.
Let these words stick to us like glue.
When you're sad or don't have a clue,
Know that self-love will always reign,
A sounding truth we all construe
To redefine ourselves again.

Love how you're made and born to do.
Be proud of how far you went through.
Empty the dark thoughts in your brain.
Rid of the old self you outgrew.
You'll redefine yourselves again.

SET V. DEPRESSION

July's Twilight

July’s tan twilight,
The dusk after summer’s light,
Sunset ‘til midnight.

Fall colors on full display!
Sunset pictures in Norway,
Northern lights wither away.
Sensational near Taipei.
Peach horizon near the bay.
Fireworks explode far away.
Tranquil drives on the highway.

July’s twin twilight,
Let the moon be my nightlight.
Skies are clear tonight.

Friendships made at the soirées.
Stargazed dreams from the driveways.
Tasted sundaes and parfaits.
Sounds of laughter, joy, and praise.
Reminisce of summer days.
Summer break became Fridays
And much-needed holidays.

Here comes the young night.
My blue star shines through the night.
Let's have a good night.

Blue Jazz

A musical jazz ballad.

Hear the music and the song of the brass!
Hear the sounds of the Blue Orleans jazz band:
Gospel, country, folk, rock, soul, and bluegrass,
Even the blues and hymns from our mainland.
Join the lit Mardi Gras parade so grand.
Let the instruments play. Let's sing along.
Come and dance 'til you sweat out your
headband.
Encourage your heart with a blue jazz song.

Tonight, my heart's scattered, shattered like glass.
A heartbreaking testimony unplanned.
My life's on paused when I reached an impasse:
Random circumstances I can't command
Watch me fall into despair like quicksand
For trying to appear alright and strong.
Sing the blues, my soul! Share your pain firsthand!
Encourage your heart with a blue jazz song.

Black jukebox jamming in the hot air mass
While we read stories from the street's newsstand.
We sing country songs through cities we pass,
Road trips and campfires, dreams of our farmland.
Rock to reggae music like a steel band.
Lyrics speak truths we love to sing along.
Dance and sweat your winter blues away and
Encourage your heart with a blue jazz song.

When I partied all night, I said, "Alas,
My depressed soul returns to the inkstand.
Write a prayer to God for a bypass,
A channel to reach for the Holy Land."
Spent my years wandering through the wasteland.

Sung hymns and gospel songs to keep me
strong.

Praised my way through, walking on a thin
strand.
Encourage your heart with a blue jazz song.
Music became my redemption lifelong,
My freedom, my sole ticket to dreamland,
A retreat of rest, a home. I belong
In this space when life's hard to understand.

Elegy to my musical lovers.

I dearly miss you all as time passes,
Singing songs together in our homeland.
But I'll sing our songs, so joy surpasses
Doubt and despair, storms I couldn't withstand.

A Dark Miracle

I. SELF-ESTEEM

I was Your dark miracle under the moonlight.
An unseen spectacle, an unbearable sight,
Living inside this broken tabernacle and losing my fight,
Falling into a cataclysmic cycle, which started on a dark night.

I slipped into a pit and fell
Into years of despair alone in my prison cell
Under this depressive spell.
Welcome to my inner hell.

I miss my cheerful side,
But isolation became my answer for a joy denied.
Like a crab, I found a shell where I could hide,
A grave to grieve my inner kid who died.

I was Your blue star on the celestial plain.
But my mistakes and sins cause You so much pain.
Now, I'm drowning in a river of thoughts in my brain,
Wondering if my existence was all in vain.

II. ISOLATION

I'm a burden too heavy to carry,
And I'm left in solitary.
You can't tolerate me, even with dairy.
I'm just a walking zombie near the cemetery.

I never fit in with the crowd,
Cause I live my life under a rain cloud.
I wish You could hear me crying out loud,
"I wish I could've made You proud."

Now I live near a dark brook,
Telling my experiences in a notebook.
I became the town's monster that left folks shook,
A tale they created to reel others in like a fish on a hook.

I became an evangelistic project for them to gloat.

A transactional relationship, a tragic story, they wrote:
How they exercise the demons from my throat
When their discouraging words spawn them inside me for a spectacle to promote.

III. DEPRESSION

Wish I could see better days,
But it's hard to discover the ways
To find happiness in the blaze,
Uninterested in things appealing to my gaze.

Sick of leaving relationships heartbroken.
Tired of fake friends and lying lovers treating my heart like a token.
Weary of speaking about a pain unspoken,
And no one cared, even when I sounded soft-spoken.

Lost my appetite to enjoy the fruits I grew.
Sick to my stomach like I have the flu.
But I'm crying and praying on a church pew,
Telling You I'm through.

Why do I hate what I become?
A monster I cannot run from.
A broken child, hopeless and glum.
Now I'm an adult, depressed and numb.

IV. DESPAIR

I come to this altar in prostration,
Seeking Your merciful salvation.
Free me from this temptation
Of falling into despair and suicidal ideation!

I'm not deserving to seek Your face.
But I know You give us strength to run this race.
But I'll take the risk, arriving near "The Most Holy Place,"
Though I'm undeserving of Your mercy and grace.

I hit rock bottom in a hard place,
Void of love and compassion here in space.
I'm a broken sinner, feeling the disgrace,
But a depressed saint, seeking Your embrace.

Hold me close so I can learn to cope.
Almost lost my life, letting go of the rope.
Will You seek me from Your telescope?
You're my first and last hope.

V. HEALING

I fail You so many times,
Thinking I didn't deserve You because of my crimes,

Working for nickels and dimes
And reacting so sour, like lemons and limes.

My story, written from Your escritoire,
Is a broken man riddled with every bloody scar.
I'm Your disappointed expectation, never reaching far.
Your hope, crushed and forgotten in an abattoir.

I hated myself, feeling I wasn't worth the care.
Left alone in the wilderness, yet You join me there,
Remind me that I'm Your child, so precious and rare.
I'm indebted to You, a vow I swear.

I won't ask You to take away this thorn
Because I would rather cry and mourn
To heal a life that's broken and torn.
I'm Your dark miracle since the day I was born.

Blue Steel

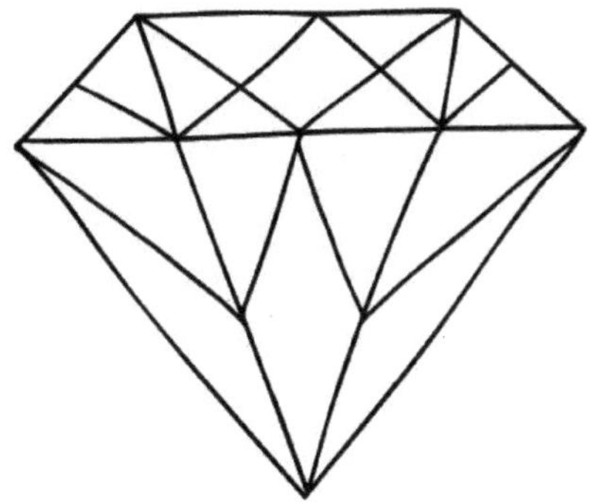

"Nobody's gonna save you
To protect your heart so blue."
But I'll share my pain to heal
My heart oxidized in steel.
My therapy and breakthrough.

My inner child's coming through,
"Nobody's gonna save you."
I'm a Black man with tough steel,
But these emotions reveal
Silent battles in dark blue.

Darkness comes to dim my light.
My dark thoughts, each restless night,
"Nobody's gonna save you."
My God, please help me pursue
A hope beautiful and bright.

Here’s my mental corrosion,
And my temple’s erosion.
Mind’s degraded from mildew.
“Nobody’s gonna save you
From this inner explosion!”

A rusted shield colored blue
Can’t protect my heart so new
Of sharing thoughts and feelings
To God beyond the ceilings,
“Nobody’s gonna save you!”

“Nobody’s gonna save you
To protect your heart so blue.”
But I’ll share my pain to heal
My heart oxidized in steel.
My therapy and breakthrough.

Dark Thoughts

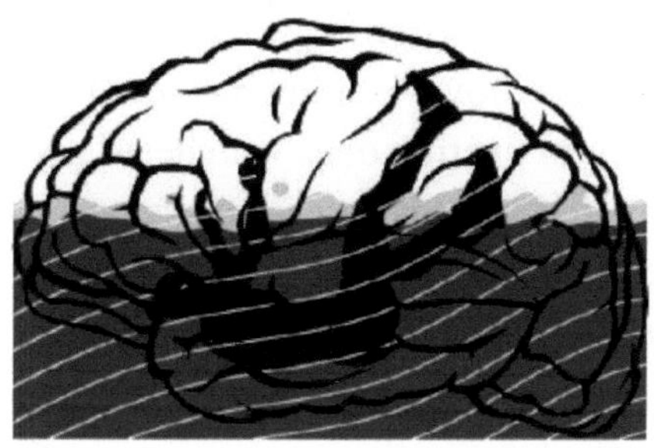

Save me from the darkness here in my head!
How the dark thoughts cover my troubled mind
In this abyss of despair, hope declined,
Scared to walk through this dark, tunneled valley?
Deprive myself of food from the galley.
Scared to run through the city's dark alley.
I'm undeserving of mercy and grace.
I've fallen over an untied shoelace.
Am I not enough, a broken disgrace?
I curse the day I was born, my birthplace.
Let me drown in this lake of misery.
Sought people to save with one simple plea.
Ignored me 'til I washed up from the sea.
Will you hear my call? Please listen to me,
Before I joined them on the hanging tree!
Why do I contemplate such dark thoughts here?
It's hard to share with people far and near.

Is my despair too sad and dark to hear?
Sick of feeling broken for one more year.
But I’m thankful, choosing to live and try.
Was this really love, helping me get by?
Thank you to the true ones who heard my cry.
I’ll find relief for this mental migraine
To ease the tempest raging in my brain.
Save me from despair living in my head!

Breathe

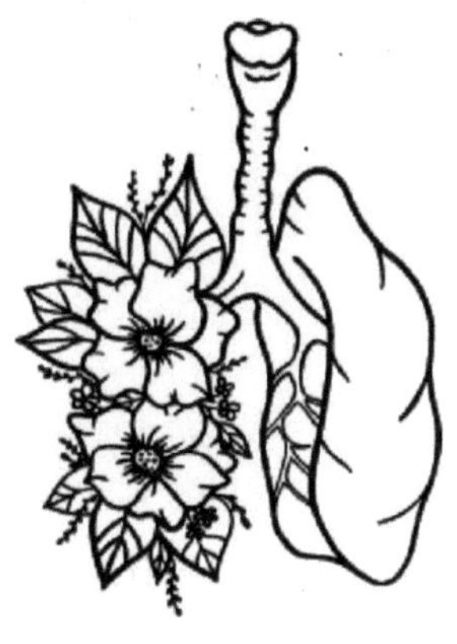

Breathe, my soul, breathe.
Rapha, please heal me, piece by piece.
Breathe, my soul, breathe.
Exhale your pain in the words you release.
Inhale hope for a masterpiece.
Be at rest in His inner peace.
Breathe, my soul, breathe.

Music

My muse, divine inspiration for creating a song.
A love language of soothing sounds, a
captivating song.

Your lyrics and instruments create original
sounds.
Divine creativity fashioned a fascinating song.

Singers and musicians use their gifts to follow
your lead.
You write, direct, and produce, coordinating
towards a song.

You have a library of genres everywhere you go,
Local and subverted sounds facilitating through
song.

How you cheer me, as I'm dancing and skating
to the beat
And break my heart with sad emotions weighing
through your song.

Encouraged me with messages, convicted me with harsh truths.
Subliminal life lessons communicating through song.

Never judged my emotions or feelings through my hard days.
Freed my soul to smile and cry, liberating me through song.

You are a cozy space, a home to calm my anxieties.
I return to my roots, concentrating on every song.

My life's playlist plays the memorable parts of my life.
Unlocked my memories, commemorating loved ones through song.

You saved and changed lives. You influenced all generations.
Your timeless legacy is about creating harmony and dissonance through song.

Gravity

An empty chair in the living room
Pierce your heart buried in a 6-foot-deep tomb.
Grief feels like gravity.

You miss a genuine friend.
Long conversations and quality time end.
Absence feels like gravity.

You can't trust your friends anymore these days.
They change so much like moon phases.
Heartbreaks feel like gravity.

Painful memories unlocked traumas.
Peeling old wounds created lifelong dramas.
Heavy suitcases feel like gravity.

You try your best to continue through life,
But it's difficult to be positive and find hope in
this dystopian world of strife.
Despair feels like gravity.

Someone comforts you, coming to you like a
descending dove.
Empathy, sympathy, compassion, and love.
Relief lightens gravity.

Hug your folks when you get a chance.
Tell them that you love them in advance.
Presence lightens gravity.

Tired of certain people giving you hell?
Free yourself from the dark cell.
Healing from heartaches lightens gravity.

Even though it hurts to remember the past,
You take those memories and lessons to
encourage you when you're downcast.
Levy your suitcase, your gravity.

Appreciate the hope you have under your blue
skies.
Perseverance and faith are the cucumbers resting
on your eyes.
Let self-care handle your gravity.

Maintenance

Mistakes we made,
Affirmations we say.
Idols we build and kill.
Notebooks we expound our thoughts.
Tears we shed and cried.
Emotions we felt.
Needs we met.
Adventures we go on.
Never forget to
Care for yourself,
Embrace self-care for personal maintenance.

Healing

Healing is like a glass of lemonade.
Bittersweet journey to break every chain.
Leave your wounds alone under the band-aid
'Till you discover what's causing your sprain.
Don't hurt yourself trying to toil and strain.
Take a road trip and enjoy the long drive.
Give your body a break, even your brain.
Healing's a journey to restore and thrive.

We're rejuvenated under the shade
To enjoy God's gifts. We dare not complain.
Let's enjoy what we have before they fade.
Peace, joy, and abundant life we obtain.
Goals and visions are rising like champagne.
Let's be grateful we're breathing and alive,
Taking vacations in the calm terrain.
Healing's a journey to restore and thrive.

When I'm done, you will see my new upgrade.
I'm minding my business in my own lane.
A masterpiece in progress that's God-made.
Pour my insecurities down the drain.
Insert the IV through every red vein.
Check the memories in my brain's archive.
Peace is my ruler, a prince who shall reign.
Healing's a journey to restore and thrive.

Healing’s a trip to keep the peace you gain,
Long-enduring hike, trying to survive.
Soon, we’ll find total healing for our pain.
Healing's a journey to restore and thrive.

SET VI. RENEWAL

Holy Refinement

God, who controls Death,
Burn my old self. Refine me
Til' I'm pure diamond.

Interment

I buried the old version of myself in the grave.
Start the processional toward the final resting place.
It's my inner child I'm hoping to save.

I shave
My beard and prepare my clothes for the nebula's embrace.
I buried the old version of myself in the grave.

Let the shooting stars carry me like a tidal wave,
Sailing to face the demons who made me a disgrace
And protecting the inner child I strived to save.

Pain and death made me a broken slave,
Until I surrender and replace
The old version of myself in the grave.

My heart, be strong and brave,
As I finish this race.
I'm reaching for the inner child I hope to save.

Bury my old self in the cave.
Until I tell Death face-to-face,
To take the old version of myself to the grave,
To free my inner child, I persevered to save.

White Dwarf

Born from dust,
A soul so captivating.
Mature, humble model one can trust.
I developed into a shining star, now graduating.

My heart carries living water like a river,
Streaming to parched deserts and terrain.
Wisdom gives me words to deliver
A message of hope to relieve the pain.

Now, I exhausted all my power and my gifts,
Living with depression.
Through navy skies, I lived with what-ifs
Until I went to the altar, sharing every imitated confession.

My young days have gone as my black hairs turn gray,
But my imagination remains, pressing me forward to the creative zone.
You can't drive me away from the stairway
That took me higher above the universe towards the Lord's throne.

I care less who talked about me in hostile fashion,
I'm not responsible for their frustration.
I'm minding my business with a divine passion
Cause God made peace my firm foundation.

My inner child still lives here,
The stories and hopes I cherish.
I hope to grow old, my dear,
Fulfilling my purpose before my body begins to perish.

Will my legacy last a million years?
Who knows what the future may hold?
I will finish this life with my eyes filled with tears,
Confident and steadfast until I reach Paradise on the narrow road made of gold.

Purple Graphs

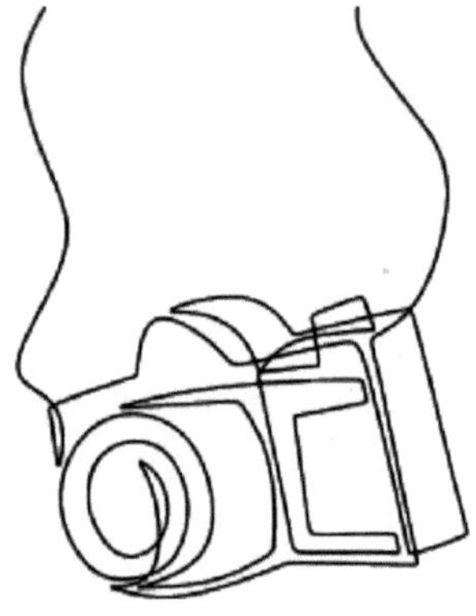

Blueprints covered red pen marks
Are the revisions of my destiny like I'm
embarking on my different character arcs.

The legendary red-blue eraser
Erases my mistakes and sins, so I can forgive
myself and move forward.

Navy jeans and a red T-shirt,
Comfortable clothes to enjoy time at the park
with a Sunday's delight sundae.

Red robins and bluejays,
My aggression and grace conflicted in response
to Life's circumstances.

Blue ice and red-hot flames,
Mixed emotions of sadness and anger when I'm
tired of manipulative games.

Cranberries and blueberries
Bring the salads and smoothies during
get-togethers with their cousins, the cherries.

Blue oceans and red sunsets
Create Nature's original art over the horizon.

Red blood and blue lakes
Gives me oxygen and strength to face the
journey ahead.

Blue and red diamonds never perish.
They're our jewels, rare memories of our
accomplishments and friendships we cherish.

Purple photographs,
A royal album of our lives told in a million
paragraphs.

Blue Skies

I. CREATION
God of the blue skies,
Bury my soul with mercy,
Your mended treasure.

Immanuel, thanks
For answering my prayer,
My close friend and muse.

Your blue star in space
Gave his all before he died
And became a dwarf.

Blueprints and visions,
Human plans, divine purpose,
And lifelong belief.

I'm a miracle,
My parents' answered prayer:
Joslyn's own brother.

II. NATURE

Morning blues no more.
Gratitude took advantage
Of the days still left.

Pursuits, dreams, and hopes
Began at this peaceful lake,
Cherished resting place.

Like coral salmon,
Through these uncharted waters,
I'll persevere through.

Like a bird or plane,
I'll fly through the sky of dreams,
A kid chasing clouds.

Each day like Sunday,
Free to enjoy peace and joy
Like a fruit sundae.

But I shed my tears
To grieve, cry, and remember
My rainy moments.

I release my rage
Like a thunderstorm in spring,
crying out my fears.

Wisdom, share your words!
Write your teachings on my heart
Like the evening dew.

Am I'm deserving
Of grace, blessings, and mercies
From Heaven above?

In every blue moon,
Be grateful for the moments
And unearned blessings.

III. IDENTITY

Wore my crown with grace.
Though it's heavy on my mind,
It's divine greatness.

Checked my reflection
To appreciate what's right
And improve what's wrong.

I rock with the blue.
Comfortable with myself.
I accept myself.

My cool energy
Comes not from clothes cool or fly.
It's my heart they love.

Ran myself away.
An emotional wreck for
Losing everything.

Couldn't find myself,
Hidden in hoodies and masks.
But I'll find myself.

Yet, I found myself
Wearing jeans as strong as faith
To know who I am.

I'm my own ICON,
Iconic and creative,
Observant and new.

Here's my VIP:
Friends who I can count on and
Folks who feel alone.

Holy Spirit, come
Let your rivers pour in me
Pure living water.

IV. RELATIONSHIPS
Lord, I praise You now,
For your wonders, works, and words,
My first only love.

I became a friend
For the ones I care about:
A kind, caring friend.

I was a lover,
A gentleman of real love
Under the blue light.

My pink lemonade,
A satisfying feeling of
Cherishing your love.

Liability
Of my own fatal mistake:
To trust the wrong one.

A broken trust hurts
Like an arctic, cold winter
Of mixed emotions.

Yet, I search for peace,
Synergy, serenity,
Forgiveness and strength.

My pen, write it down:
My experiences and hopes,
My darkness and pains.

Strengthen my strong roots,
So I can cut dead branches
And burn them away.

I'm healing inside
Through my mirrored reflection
To be who I am.

V. DEPRESSION

In July's twilight,
I paint the night to have fun
On a summer night.

I keep myself warm,
Embraced with autumn's dance and
The sounds of blue jazz.

I went through winters
To share my cold despair as
Your dark miracle.

Did not blue the steel.
Exposed the rotten pieces
Through deep spring cleaning.

Dealing with dark thoughts,
Drowning in my brain of my
Hidden brokenness.

I just need to breathe,
O, let my soul be freed from
These mixed emotions.

Music, soothe my soul
With songs, tunes, and melodies:
Your long legacy.

In each dark moment,
Let gravity take me 'til
I reach rock bottom.

Need home maintenance:
Self-care renovations for
Healing this blue soul.

I will rest today,
Relieve my brain's mental toil,
Heal my broken soul.

VI. RENEWAL
Refine, purify
'Til I'm strong as a diamond,
A brand-new creature.

Let the dead self die.
Death is the new birth of hope
Where an old dream died.

Though I grow older,
I matured to cherish hope,
Gained wisdom and faith.

Cherish these moments.
The blessings of the blue skies
Found in purple graphs.

Cloudy or stormy,
I'm thankful for my blue skies,
My lifelong forecast.

9 789363 310452

Printed by Libri Plureos GmbH in Hamburg,
Germany